flowers by design

PHOTOGRAPHY BY DAVID LOFTUS

JEFF LEATHAM

FLOWERS BY DESIGN

An imprint of HarperCollins*Publishers*

FLOWERS BY DESIGN

Text copyright © 2003 by Jeff Leatham
All photography copyright © 2003 by David Loftus

First published in the United States in 2004 by
Harper Design International
An imprint of HarperCollins*Publishers*
10 East 53rd Street
New York, NY 10022

First published in Great Britain in 2003 by
PAVILION BOOKS

An imprint of **Chrysalis** Books Group plc

The Chrysalis Building, Bramley Road
London W10 6SP

The moral right of the author has been asserted.

Design: Paul Welti
Commissioning editor: Kate Oldfield
Assistant editors: Katherine Morton and Mary
Macnaghten
Location research: Jess Walton

HarperCollins books may be purchased for
educational, business or sales promotional use. For
information, please write:
Special Markets Department, HarperCollins*Publishers*
Inc., 10 East 53rd Street, New York, NY 10022.

Colour reproduction at Classic Scan Pte Ltd.
Printed and bound at SNP Leefung, China

1 2 3 4 5 6 7 8 9 10 / 10 09 08 07 06 05 04

Library of Congress Control Number: 2003109861

ISBN: 0-06-059275-3

CONTENTS

To my Father,
who taught me as a child
the beauty of art and nature
and how to enjoy all that was around me.
His great talent for mixing colour and shape
turned my childhood
into a fantasy for the senses
which opened my mind
to the world that I now live in.

MY PHILOSOPHY

To experience eye-catching cut flowers is to stimulate the senses. Flowers appeal to everyone and thus they can act as a sensual liaison between people and the space in which they live or work. Flowers can totally change a room, both in mood and focus, according to colour, season, quality of light and occasion. And yet so many people overlook these facts. How often does the half-hearted, wilting display of flowers belie the design effort that has been put into the decorative scheme of the room?

Flowers are *the* new element in interior design. Effective display can accentuate architectural features, imitate pattern and style, herald the seasons and bring a decorative scheme to life.

My work is about striking form, using one or two colours and strong, sculptural shapes. It is about bold statements, using the lines of the flower, chic containers, and sometimes an abundance of one flower for dramatic effect. The key word here is sculpture – the art of celebrating form. I seek to reveal the flower; drawing dramatic attention to its colour, its delicacy and its strength.

It is important to relate to a space. Free your mind of preconceived notions and react intuitively. Be inspired by the quality of light and the proportions of the room. Respond to your own mood.

To demonstrate how this can be achieved this book is split into two parts. The first sets out the basic principles; the second puts theory into practice. The striking results are due in great part to the beauty and chic style of the homes in which we worked. Inspiration came easily and the success of each display makes the irrefutable case that flower design can appear to be part of the room's original conception.

the new interior element

DESIGN
BASICS

INTRODUCING THE NEW STYLE

Long-stemmed "Grand Prix" roses tipped at an angle to establish an astonishing focal point [RIGHT] encapsulate my work perfectly. I am fortunate to have an intuitive response to the space around me but that is not all that feeds my inspiration. The confidence to know what will work comes with practice. I often begin one idea only to ditch it and let a new design appear. I respond to the shape, light and colours of a room. Thus, in a room such as this contemporary space, which is dominated by regular square shapes, a strong group of "tipped-to-tumble" roses creates the perfect foil. The design is anchored by three rose heads floating in asymmetric glass bowls beneath the glass of the table. They act as vivid punctuation marks among otherwise massive shapes.

HOW TO APPROACH A ROOM

It is important to work with your space, not against it. So, first principles come into play. Evaluate your space before even thinking about the flowers. Look around. Assess where flowers might be placed. Consider what container might be appropriate. The vase will play a big part in the overall scheme. It will provide support and maintain the shape and strength of your work, while forming part of your display.

analyze the light source

Are you working with natural daylight, artificial light or candlelight? Will that light source and quality change dramatically during the day and into the evening?

Finally, think about the colour and size of the room and decide what effect you want to achieve – I tend to follow my moods – I may decide to load a dark room with terrible portentous colour for a gothic effect or I might simply lift the shadows with the purest whites. The choice is yours. Now pick your flowers.

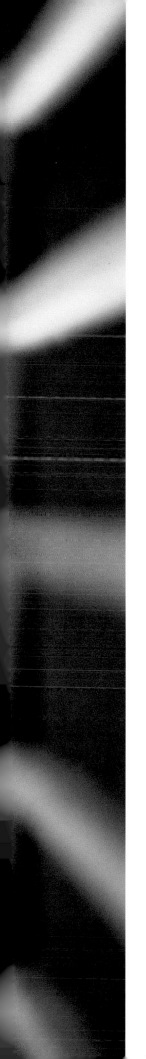

move around

Creating bold designs can be an intimidating task. The key to success is to take the space and furnishings into consideration.

As you begin to work, take time to stand back and observe all aspects of the room. Think about how it will be seen from different viewpoints. The architectural features of your room will form the stage for your performance.

As they are transitional spaces, staircases and corridors allow your flowers to be seen from many different angles. I kept the ascent of the viewer in mind when I placed the cobalt-blue hydrangeas at the bottom of this wide wooden staircase [LEFT AND RIGHT]. At first, as you approach the display at eye level, you are not aware that a riot of burnt orange "Naranga" rose heads jostle at the top of the vase – a point which becomes clear as you mount the stairs.

From above, the strong interplay of the two complementary colours is easily observed.

Single or multiple flowers displayed out of water is one of my signature statements. Displaying them in this way accentuates the form of the flower. Calla lilies (*Zantedeschia aethiopica*) are perfect for this treatment – I would include them on my list of signature flowers – as are the carnations seen above. A list of suitable flowers that can last out of water for up to four or five hours (to take them easily through a party) can be found on page 154.

keep it simple

The pattern of Casablanca lilies
brings simple texture and contrast to
the elegance of a minimalist room.

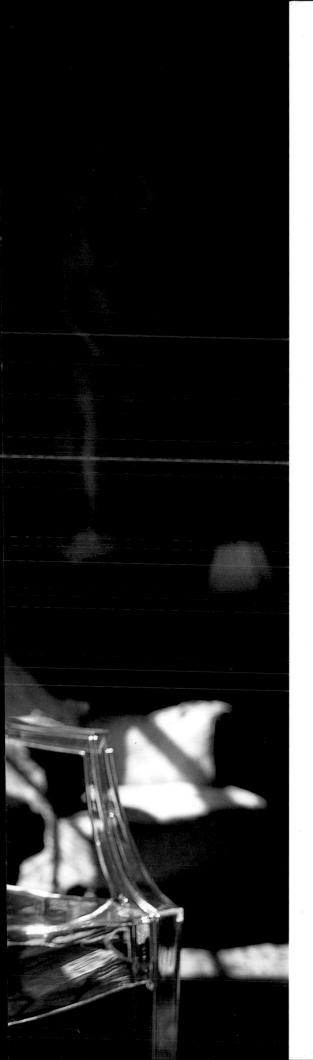

let light be your guide

A window is a perfect opportunity
for display. The direct light source
brings drama to your composition.
And throughout the day and into the
evening the colours of your flowers
will be changed by the pale cold
light of dawn, the bright glare of the
midday sun and then the bathing
glow of evening.

This composition of orange
Fritillaria imperialis
befits the style of the
18th-century shuttered
room. The modern "Louis ghost"
chair echoes the transparent vase
and adds a touch of wit to an
otherwise period piece.

sculptural forms

For a dramatic impact, take liberties
with form. Think of yourself as a
sculptor working with a three-
dimensional object to be viewed
from all directions. When
considering form bring petals,
stems and even bulbs and roots into
play. Adding raw nature to your
space – here I've used hyacinth
bulbs – brings in a bold element.

cubism

If the room is your canvas and the flowers are your paints, then the vase is your paintbrush. In other words, it is essential to build a range of containers in different colours and shapes in which to display your creations.

You will need vases for long stems and height, globes
for trapping gorgeous blossom. Look for styles that suit
your decor. I often use multiples of the same shape to
create rhythm and pace in my work. A useful and
beautiful collection can be built up slowly over the years.

DROWNINGS AND DRENCHINGS

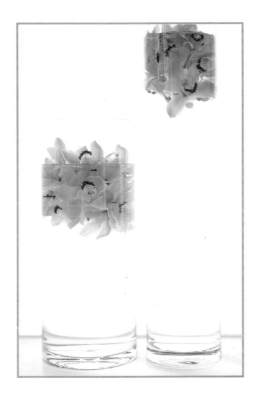

Another signature composition of my work is to "drown" flowers, completely submerging them to magnify their perfections. Topping up your vase with sparkling water will create hundreds of tiny bubbles that cling to the petals and stems for up to three days. A list of flowers that can be used for this treatment appears on page 154. Here I have designed with orange calla lillies (*Zantedeschia aethiopica*) [LEFT] and [ABOVE, CLOCKWISE FROM BOTTOM LEFT] green cymbidium orchids, yellow tulips and gold calla lillies.

theory into practice

FLOWER
SPACES

WORKING WITH LIGHT

Light is one of our most precious resources when it comes to design. A good eye learns to harness its myriad qualities and use them to better display flowers' beauty. And, of course, shadows are important too: note the chiaroscuro (an art term meaning "light and shade") of the narcissus opposite.

The boldness of white in an otherwise dark room brings a subtle emphasis to the contrast of natural daylight and dark wood tones. This and the following pages represent a composition of opposites: dark and light; baroque spirals and simplicity; heavy decor and an ethereal display of gypsophila. In the "hierarchy of chic" white is the most simple (compare with the use of black on page 116). Gypsophila ("baby's breath"), often considered a cliché "filler" for bouquets, is both affordable and looks wonderful used alone and in a large mass.

The simple act of bringing flowers
into a room immediately imparts a
sensuality to the space that provokes
a passionate response in the viewer.
Often bold simplicity can have a

white is the simplest colour to
work with – it will please all tastes

great impact – actively engaging the
eye of the beholder. Here masses of
white gypsophila [LEFT] and narcissus
[ABOVE] balance the heavy shadows of
the interior.

light and shade

Flowers were used in this environment to encourage movement down the shadowy passage to the small day room at the end. This was done by setting two glass globes on top of each other and filling the upper one to bursting with wild summer-coloured poppies. The arrangement sits in a pool of light and beckons like a beacon along the corridor.

The exotic and ornamental opium poppy (*Papaver somniferum*) was chosen for its timeless beauty to bring a Vermeer-like calm to this scene in a 17th-century London townhouse.

Two assertive arrangements of long-stemmed "Jacaranda" roses stand tall in a flag-stoned basement. The play of light through the stems and water creates a sun-dial effect on the floor as the hours pass. This arrangement needs colour as accent so as not to be overpowered by the room's utilitarian pale colours. The opulence of roses works well as a contrast to the simplicity of the rustic surroundings.

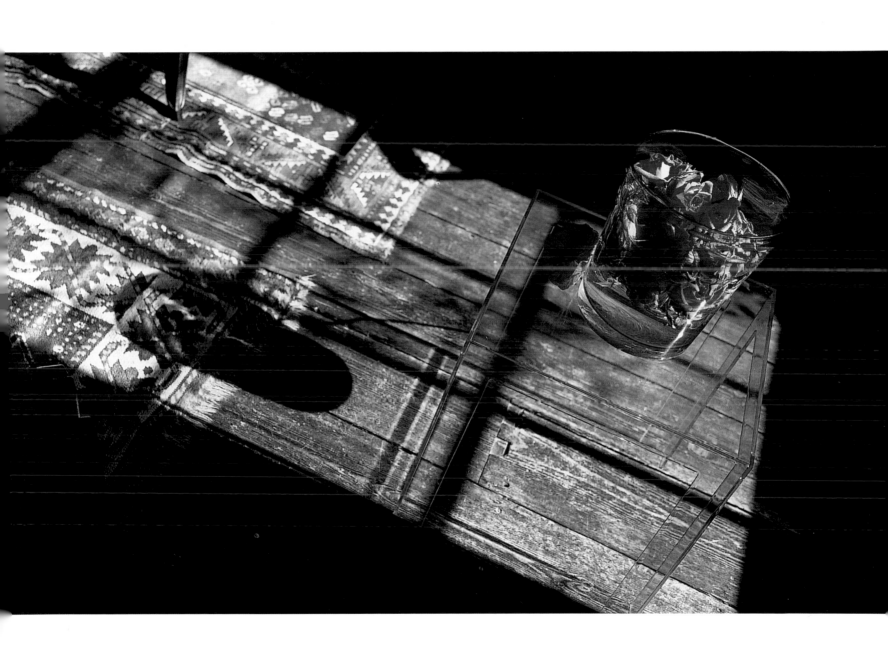

bright light, bright colour

The owners of this light-doused contemporary space are lucky to have such a large amount of sunlight entering their apartment, considering the crowded urban environment in which it is located.

the use of bright statement colour in a light and white modern interior

The broad abundance of light and space available lends itself to larger statements. For example, the forsythia "wall" along the windows and the large bowl of "mango" burnt-orange calla lilies on the table (for flowers that can be displayed out of water, see pages 24–25).

thinking as a child

Strong colour and bold stylistic themes are an invitation to design with a palette of primary hues. A safe flower choice would have been white but this room can take the "pop" of colour – provided by the "Yokohama" tulips shown here – to balance the 1950s–style glass weights on the table.

creating a bold statement

The key to making generous
proportions of flowers work is to
use a single colour. It creates a
monumentality that is impossible to
forget. In a dark, shadowy space
such as this you need to make a
screaming statement with bright
colour. Here a single green and white

when you think there is enough,
just add a little bit more

Maudiae orchid (*Paphiopedilum
maudiae*) augments and contrasts
with the shock of fiery orange
"dinner plate" dahlias and
"Malaga" orange carnations [RIGHT].
In this interior it was essential to use
one colour to counterbalance the
eclectic decorative scheme. The
whole display is wedded with a soft
deep layer of "Milva" orange
rose petals [ABOVE].

artificial light

The effect of artificial light is much more defining and unforgiving. It brings strong shadows into play and allows you to experiment with form until you achieve the pattern you require. For a more dramatic look try simple but pronounced forms such as gold calla lilies [ABOVE] or curly bamboo [RIGHT].

stealing the limelight

Use lighting to create drama. In a
dark, tapestry-hung interior, a single
slipper orchid (*Paphiopedilum*)
becomes a focal point when

knowing how to use light to
your advantage is the key to
many creative ideas

highlighted with a focused beam of
rich artificial light. The effect makes
the waxy petals of the orchid appear
almost as porcelain, turning nature
into art.

This effect can be imitated by
using downlighters in niches and
architectural recesses.

candlelight

The light cast by candles has a sexy glow and is therefore perfect for a seductive supper. Control and excess are the key to seduction – the expert knows when to stop. What could pave the way to passion better than a table overflowing with the petals and heads of deep red roses *Rosa* "Grand Prix" and *Rosa* "Black Beauty", crimson carnations, orange calla lilies and candles?

COMPOSITION

When planning how to use flowers
in an interior first think about where
your containers should stand. There
are two focal points in this room:
one at standing eye-level and one at
seated eye-level. In general, no room
should have more than two floral
focal points.

creating focal points

Then think about composition:
choose shapes that will be visually
imposing. You can create a dramatic
reaction by using forms that cause
surprise. In this room, which is
decorated with classical restraint,
the angle of the long branches of
Ilex forms an ironic counterpoint to
the overriding formality of the room.
The drowned berry-covered holly
also flouts tradition.

creating conversation pieces

The three elements that
appear above this table –
picture, plates and glass light
– are brought into a cohesive
grouping in the eye of the
beholder as the three lines
of fuschia Guernsey lily

use accent colour to
turn a group of items into
a conversation piece

(*Nerine sarniensis*) lead the
eye around the composition,
discouraging the eye from
resting in any one place.

accenting signature pieces

Less is more: use brightly coloured, precious, long-stemmed flowers – such as this brightly toned *Phalaenopsis* orchid – to accent a signature piece and bring new focus to a room.

FORMS

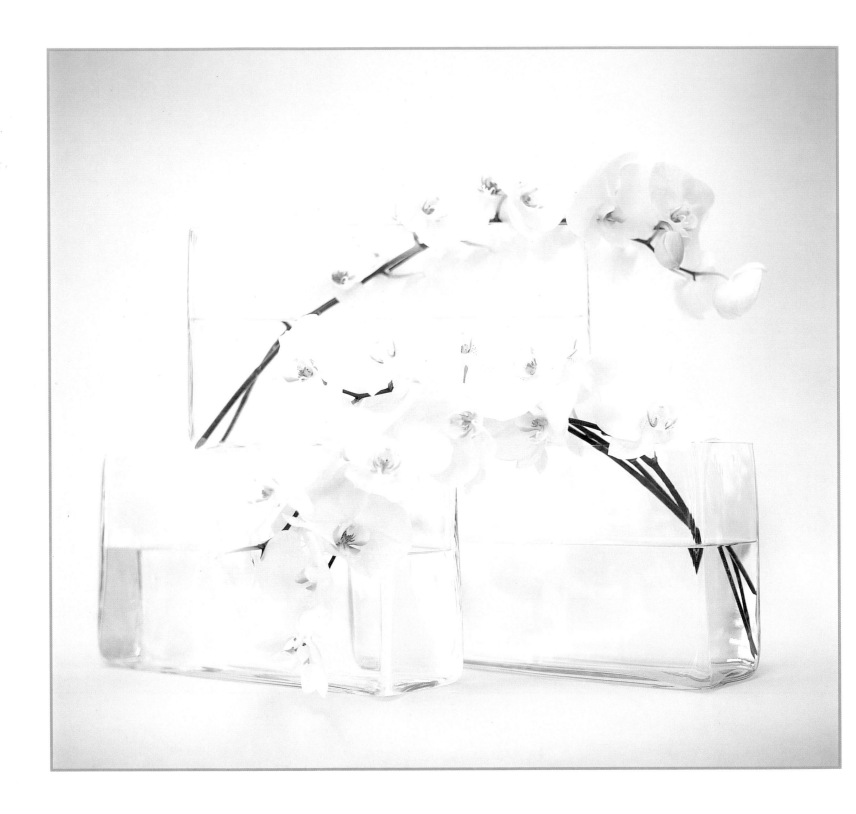

One aspect that distinguishes my work is the way in which flowers follow the lines and curves of the vase. Designing with the shape of the vase in mind simplifies the design process. Allowing the stems to balance against the side of the vase – a trademark of mine – gives an architectural feeling to my arrangements.

linking form to furniture

In many ways successful design is
about successful partnerships. In
this home we brought contrasting
shapes and texture to the fore by
using yellow "kangaroo paw"
(*Anigozanthos*) at an angle beneath
the circular pierced opening.
This slanting wiry composition
seeks to link the aperture to the
contemporary "Eros" chair placed in
the foreground.

When you are working do not
be afraid to move your furniture
around to suit your flowers – it
doesn't always have to be the other
way around.

amassing colour

This retro fantasy room uses
bold orange and pink to balance the
wide sweeps of colour in the room's
decor. When confronted by strong
colours try using clashing tones with
simple masses of a single colour –
such as these pink hydrangeas – to
bring the scheme to life. "Blue
Magic" *Vanda* orchids and single-
stem *Cattleya* orchids (on the table
in the centre of the room) cannot be
matched for their sheer joyous
lipstick vibrancy.

"Jeff's arrangements
and floral designs have
influenced the floral arrangements
in my home. His designs are unusually
refreshing and very inspiring."

TINA TURNER

using flowers as sculpture

When the whole flower is beautiful
why hide most of its body? Don't
forget the stem – so many people do.
When devising a display keep the
line of long-stemmed flowers in
mind. The stems, arching against
the vase, speak for themselves. Here,
white calla lilies (accompanied by
white orchids in the foreground),
tipping out of a vase or plunging
head-first under water, look as
graceful as they do in nature.

Consider new placement for your containers. Larger vases can stand in the middle of a room, since the weight of water in them will make them quite stable. Grouping or pairing vases will ensure rewarding comparisons between the flowers on display.

Cube and globe vases create the perfect opportunity to bend and twist long-stemmed flowers, such as these mini white "Crystal Blush" calla lilies, allowing the water and glass to create optical illusions when viewed from different angles. Even if the base of the stem is not in the water the flower remains hydrated.

STYLE

Once you have decided how to deal with the basic elements of flower design (light, container, composition and placement), you will want to pick your flowers. Allow the style of the room to inspire you, suggesting colour, shape and kind of flower. Occasionally it is rewarding to reflect the decoration quite literally, as in the pink lotus flowers and green lotus pods chosen for this urban loft kitchen, inspired by the Indian paintings that adorn the walls.

Simplicity is chic. This simple but monumental interior was treated with a monochromatic design. The five white anthuriums spring from two upright vases and are anchored by the contrasting circular form of a heavy ceramic bowl filled with white carnation heads. The texture of the waxy anthuriums appears exaggerated against the matt surface of the bowl in a perfect exercise in harmony and balance.

same room...

Black calla lilies and "Queen of the Night" tulips bring drama to a pale, streamlined interior. I used more traditionally luxurious flowers in this room as a contrast to the modernity of the architecture.

You may decide to keep your favourite colour palette as a signature statement. Here are two examples of using the same colour through different flowers – calla lilies and tulips [LEFT] and two bunches of "Black Beauty" roses [ABOVE].

...same vase

A cluster of vases can be as important to the composition as the flowers themselves. If the vases are beautiful in their own right, it is not essential to fill them all (see also previous page). This page shows the same vases but this time containing "Blue Magic" *Vanda* orchids.

Change the impact and focal point by playing with form and space. In the largest vases a single orchid flower floats independently.

outdoing the decor

In total contrast to the previous
interiors, the challenge of
adorning this room with flowers
was one of strength of statement.
   Surrounded by many different
objects a small composition
would have disappeared. Flowers
in this room needed to shout
out their presence, so another
layer of opulence was added to
this highly dressed interior. The
groups of flowers – purple
hydrangeas, purple delphiniums
and pink *cattleya* orchids – were
so large that they became part of
the room's furniture and had to
be negotiated accordingly.

understated opulence

No floral composition could
compete with the giant Chinese
vase in the corner so
understatement was the answer.
   Using the same flower as in the
foreground of the previous
spread – purple hydrangeas – a
small, simple display was created
in a small bowl at seated
eye-level for quiet contemplation.

VASES

Don't choose the vase for the flower, choose the flower for the vase. Look for vases that accessorize each other – multiples add strength to your design. Seek out oversized vases; pairs that complement each other; shapes such as cubes or bowls for stacking; and single-stem vases for bathrooms, bedside tables and tight budgets. I mostly use transparent containers because I love the visual effect of the stems in the water.

EMULATING PATTERN

When working with significant features in your space, be it architecture, colour, texture or pattern, experiment with "knitting" the forms and textures of your flower display into the scheme itself.

The chinoiserie of this room – the painted silk wallpaper, the ornate frame and the brain coral – cried out for the delicacy of lily of the valley (*Convallaria* "Fortin's Giant") and the rawness of its revealed roots (maintained by standing the roots in an inch or so of water).

1065433185

"Jeff's work
embodies my love of colours,
textures and shapes as he draws
voluptuously and sensuously from
a pastiche vocabulary of flowers and
foliage, veritably akin to the Garden
of Eden. He is a master at creating
mystery and beauty and above all, sign-
of-the-times elegance with the
lightest of touches."
EMANUEL UNGARO

The roots of plants are usually kept hidden but often they are the most beautiful part (see the water plants above). Revealing what is usually hidden can bring a raw organic quality to your designs. Experiment with different looks: try the ghost-like tendrils of lily of the valley or the stark white roots of a washed hyacinth bulb. Planting orchids in a glass container reveals when the plant needs water (see page 154 for a list of suggestions).

THE SEASONS

On a dismal winter day bring the prospect of spring into your home. A simple mass of yellow tulips (*Tulipa* "Yokohama") in the depths of winter creates the illusion of a spring morning. Here the same number of stems is used in these multi-holed vases as there would be in a bold bunch of flowers, creating the illusion of a field of flowers. The brightness of the tulips in this shadowy corridor makes the perfect pathway to the light-filled bedroom and prefigures the colour of the decorative scheme.

the summer sun

When the days are hotter and
there is more colour in nature it
is time to dress our homes with
flowers in a looser, more natural
fashion. Simplify your designs
with fresher-looking, hardier
flowers such as these "Green
Goddess" calla lilies.

In this space-lined interior the
surface of the kitchen counter
continues visually without a
break to the garden. This created
the perfect opportunity to design
with a row of twelve identical
oversized vases, which serve,
literally, to bring the outside in.
The design is reflected in the
outside glass, provoking a double
take reaction.

room outside

People often forget to use their outside space for the display of cut flowers. It is a perfect way of dressing "another room" of your home for a party or other special occasion.

Placing these new fushia peonies directly in the sunlight helped their tight buds open more quickly. This technique also helps with other varieties of new flowers.

autumn

Flowers and plants don't always need to come from the flower market. Who is not moved by the glow of russet colours around us signalling summer's end? This mix

signalling the changing seasons

of green and orange leaves and berries, collected on a weekend walk, reflects the changing seasons outside the home. This oversized arrangement of autumnal leaves towers over the dinner guests below.

winter

When choosing colours of flowers to use in a room you can work either against the decor (see pages 76–77) or with it. This room uses two main points of colour reference: browns and ice blues. Here the warmth of purple-berried branches of *Callicarpa* is paired with colder blues and hazy violet. A dark purple was chosen in order to maintain the tranquil rationale of the room. In order to avoid a traditional approach, the flowers are arranged at an angle and stand on a mirrored table. Therefore, as you approach the centre of the room, the number of flowers appears to increase (see also pages 126 and 128). The overall effect created is one of chic simplicity.

The colour black has become the epitome of chic – this has now extended to the use of flowers. Black creates the ultimate drama in a room. Here black-berried privet branches (*Ligustrum vulgare*) are combined with black chocolate cosmos. Black does not reflect light but seems to soak it up; massing black flowers creates points of dark, elegant intrigue in a room. (Compare this with the use of white on pages 38–41).

FOLIAGE

The addition of foliage is not a feature of my style but I do use it alone in displays or as an accent to another arrangement. I tend to use a limited range of plants, often opting for viburnum [BOTTOM LEFT], umbrella ferns [FAR RIGHT] and giant waxy-leaved anthuriums (*Anthurium clarinervium*) [TOP LEFT] for dramatic effect. Drenching anthuriums [TOP RIGHT] is a great way to magnify the strong pattern of lines. Lotus pods [BOTTOM RIGHT], coupled with cheeseplant leaves (*Monstera deliciosa*), are another favourite.

designing with the exterior in mind

This urban apartment benefits from having huge glass walls and doors that pull right back, lessening the differentiation between outside and in. This created the perfect opportunity to balance the room with the outside aesthetic.

The goal for this apartment was to bring nature indoors and to add "life" to the harshness of the cement floor and walls. The breadth of the windows easily allows the eye to make the transition from the plants indoors to the green of the trees and ferns on the patio (see pages 122-123).

A two-colour scheme was chosen for subtlety. Hints of green and white – white dahlias, "Green Goddess" calla lilies and water plants – foreshadow the real story that goes on outside.

It is important to design for all the senses. Gardenias were floated in a broad dish on the floor, not only to bring their exquisite perfume to the otherwise ascetic environment in this home, but also to soften the harsh concrete lines on the floor tiles.

REFLECTIONS

Treat yourself to a private display somewhere in your home that you pass frequently but others might not see. Ring the changes and opt for a casual and loose arrangement that looks as if your flowers have just been brought in from the garden or the market. In this shady scullery wild field flowers – muscari and Persian poppies – remain untailored and relaxed. They are carefully placed by a mirror so that the muscari are revealed to the viewer from several angles.

Making your displays an integral part of your interior design strengthens the overall impact when you walk into a room. Use elements from your decorative scheme. Mirrors are the perfect medium for dramatic display and help to create a playful interplay between form and design. Placing two vases upon a mirror reveals a secret side to this display of deep-purple *Callicarpa* berries (featured also on page 114). As you approach the centre of the room an illusion is created of a growing number of flowers.

By placing your designs in front of a mirror, as shown, the flowers become visible from several parts of the room.

mirrors can play an important role in your flower designs – tripling the original effect

Keep in mind that when designing with mirrors, the arrangement should not have an obvious front or back. The perfection of these "Avalanche" roses is shown off perfectly by this mirror.

CHANGING
TABLES

A display of flowers is the perfect dressing for an unlaid table. Tables provide the ideal platform on which to display a changing scene that reflects your mood, your style, the season or the occasion.

In this impressive 17th-century dining room traditional "Jacaranda" roses lie jauntily across modern plastic vases, defying convention.

A simple way of changing the mood of a room is to use the same arrangement of vases but change the flowers. In this high-ceilinged townhouse apartment the ornate Venetian glass vases, 17th-century chairs and unique tree-stump table are quietly matched by four regular groups of flowers: russet calla lilies [ABOVE] and viburnum [RIGHT].

The mood and feeling of a light urban loft space can easily be changed with the use of containers and different colours. (Compare with the following pages.) The minimal retro feel of this sitting area in Hoxton, London, uses a transparent fabric to divide the space. The fabric provides the perfect backdrop against which to display these "Ronaldo" tulips.

" Jeff's work is

so beautiful and flawless that

I feel a rush of endorphins whenever I'm

in its presence. I love his magical scenes

which he creates through what appears to be an

effortless blending of colour, dimension and

texture. He is a gifted artist who truly

breaks traditional notions of beauty."

JANET JACKSON

The lightness of the lilac befits the
ethereal quality of the room.
Candlelight is ushering in the
evening as the intense daylight fades
from the room.

BEHIND CLOSED DOORS

The most important place for flowers, for me, is next to the bed. Indeed the most intimate sensual connection is made possible by placing flowers in private spaces such as your bedroom or bathroom (see the rose petals extravaganza on the previous spread).

In this room a visual link is formed between the globe of white "Akito" roses and the lamp. The scent of tuberose fills the room.

"Jeff has succeeded in being

original and innovative but never loses sight

of the fact that it is the intrinsic beauty of the

flowers themselves that shine through –

he is a unique talent."

DAVID COLLINS

using opposite colours

To make a small statement
come alive use flowers of the
opposite colour in the colour
wheel to your decor. Here
purple freesias are
complementary in colour to
the impressive gold backdrop
to the bed.

In this large, formal bedroom flowers are used to highlight the three major spaces of the room – the bedside, the central table and the sitting area in the foreground. Purple *Vanda* orchids (by the bedside) and black calla lilies were chosen to echo the dark purple colour of the sofa and the glass bowl on the table.

single-stem simplicity

One last thought. One stem of your favourite flower can be as effective visually as a voluminous bouquet, while costing you far less. Single-stem statements should not be relegated to the bathroom. Choose one or more slim vases, add interesting stems such as these *Allium sphaerocephalon*, and fashion a new concept for a mantelpiece, a dining table or a hallway.

FLOWERS BY USE

The list below details flowers that are suitable for each of my design techniques. Although you do not have to stick rigidly to my suggestions, it is important to understand the types of flowers that can withstand the various treatments. I have also listed my favourite colour combinations for different seasons and flowers that you can buy on a limited budget.

NOT ALL FLOWERS NEED WATER
Most varieties of flowers will last two to three days out of water but it is important to let them have a drink for one hour per day to rehydrate the flower.
- Calla lilies (also known as arum lilies)
- Carnations
- Orchids
- Anthuriums

ROOTS
- Hyacinths with bulbs
- Tulips with bulbs
- Orchid plants
- Floating aquatic plants

BULBS
- Tulips
- Hyacinths
- Narcissi
- Amaryllis

DROWNINGS AND DRENCHINGS
- Hydrangeas
- Orchids
- Tulips
- Rose heads
- Calla lilies
- Blooming branches
- Seasonal berried branches

FLOATING FLOWER HEADS
- Roses
- Tulips
- Orchids
- Delphiniums
- Gardenias
- Peonies
- Lotus flowers

BENDABLE STEMS FOR SHAPE AND FORM
- Calla lilies
- Tulips
- Orchids

TIPPED FLOWERS
(Hearty-stemmed flowers are best)
- Long-stemmed roses
- Calla lilies
- Hydrangeas
- Lilacs
- Allium
- Eremerus
- Viburnum

FOLIAGE
- Viburnum
- Monstera (cheeseplant) leaves
- Different kinds of anthurium leaves
- Elephant ear's leaves
- Lotus pods

FAVOURITE FLOWERS FOR A LIMITED BUDGET
- Carnations
- Gypsophila (baby's breath)
- Gladioli
- Anthuriums
- Tulips
- Freesias
- Dahlias
- Gerbera
- Iris
- Anemones
- Chrysanthemums

COLOUR COMBINATIONS
When mixing colours, I tend to stick with safer monochromatic or complementary colour schemes.

Bear in mind that there are no specific rules concerning colour combinations in relation to seasons; remember too that a simple change of colour can entirely change the mood of the home.

Try to avoid mixing white with vibrant colours (eg orange and red) as white has a tendency to dominate and become the focal point of the design

SUBTLE SPRING COLOURS
Fresh greens mixed with tones of white give unfailing simplicity. Pale pinks with soft lavenders reflect feminine beauty.

REFRESHING, VIBRANT COLOURS OF SUMMER
Brilliant yellows and oranges together with green create a bold, fresh statement synonymous with the summer season.

CHIC, MYSTERIOUS COLOURS OF AUTUMN
Blacks and rich chocolate tones mixed with deep oranges bring the warmth of autumn inside.

PASSIONATE COLOURS FOR WINTER
Hot fuchsias combined with purplish blues, luscious reds and blacks bring life and intrigue to an otherwise dismal season.

A display is only as good as the quality of flowers used. Never underestimate the importance of buying freshly cut, high–quality flowers. Their impact will be greater and they will last for longer. The author and publisher would like to give special thanks to Marc Boers of Flex Holland BV, who provided the flowers seen throughout this book. Located in the renowned flower auction at Aalsmeer in the Netherlands, the company exports unsurpassed, freshly cut flowers and foliage worldwide.

For further information, please visit:
www.marcboerstrading.com
tel: +31 653 297 351
fax: +31 725 725 858

Jeff's designs require contemporary and imaginative vases. The author and publisher would like to give special thanks to Christine Brady at LSA International, who provided the majority of vases seen in this book. The collection is available in many shops throughout the UK, across Europe and in selected retailers worldwide.

For further information, please visit:
www.lsa-international.com

The author would like to thank the following for their work on the book: Kate Oldfield, Vivien James, Katherine Morton, Mary Macnaghten, Oliver Jeffreys and Zoe Nobes at Pavilion Books; Paul Welti for the design; David Loftus and his assistants Steve Griffin and Gemma Watts for the photography; Jess Walton for location research and Annabelle Oldfield for additional styling.

The book would not have been possible without those who generously let us into their beautiful homes to shoot the photography. Thanks therefore to Paul Brewster and Shaun Clarkson for the use of their flat on pages 17-19, 50-53, 71, 84-5, 128-9, 136-7, 138-9, 140-141, 148-9, (paul@brewster-style.com or www.shaunclarkson.com); David Collins; Ian Watson; Julian Land; Jane and Chris Noraika and all at Zownir; Lucia Silver (for more information please see below); Catherine and John Pawson; Hassan Abdullah; Michel Lasserre and Stefan Karlsson at Les Trois Garçons (www.lestroisgarcons.com) and Richard Sinclair at The Warehouse.

Thanks also to Purves and Purves (www.purves.co.uk) and Bo/Paris (boutique-bo@wannadoo.fr) for props; Lucia Silver's The L Boutique (lucia@thelboutique.com); Four Seasons Hotels and Resorts (www.fourseasons.com); Four Seasons Hotel George V; Leonard Hotel and Residence, London (www.theleonard.com); Covent Garden Flower Market and Metro Photo Processing/Chelsea.

Finally, the author would like to thank the following people for their help and support throughout: the Leatham family, Paul Mather, Shannon Raymond, Arabella Stirling, Paige Dixon, Natalie Smith, Lotte Oldfield, Silvi McCellan and the Studio Fleur Paris.